An Animal Abecedarium

A marvelous menagerie from AXOLOTL to ZORIL

Kristina A. Larson

Goose River Press
Waldoboro, Maine

Copyright © 2017 Kristina A. Larson.

All rights reserved. No part of this book may be reproduced in any form without written permission from the publisher, except by a reviewer who may quote brief passages in a review to be printed in a newspaper or magazine.

Library of Congress Card Number: 2017933517

ISBN: 978-1-59713-177-3

First Printing, 2017

Published by
Goose River Press
3400 Friendship Road
Waldoboro ME 04572
e-mail: gooseriverpress@roadrunner.com
www.gooseriverpress.com

An Animal Abecedarium

Axolotl with a bottle

Axolotl

Most of these unusual salamanders remain in their young, or larval, stage. They could be called the "Peter Pans" of the amphibian world! They can develop lungs if they remain in a dry place for a long period of time.

Babirusa listening to Sousa

Babirusa

This pig-like creature is also known as the "pig-deer," but some experts believe it may be more related to the hippopotamus. The male's upper tusks grow through the upper part of the snout, curving up and back to the head. There is even a legend that babirusas sleep hanging off branches by their tusks!

Cavy
in the Navy

Cavy

Simply another term for the popular pet known as the guinea pig, wild cavies originate not from Guinea but from South America. Like actual pigs, the males are called "boars" and the females "sows," but the young are usually called "pups."

Drill
with a bill

Drill

Like other monkeys, drills use many facial expressions to communicate. When a drill shows its teeth in a grin, it is a friendly gesture, where in other primates it is often a sign of aggression. Drills live in large groups which can merge with others, totalling over 200 individuals. Their entire world range is smaller than the state of West Virginia.

Eider
guzzling cider

Eider

Most people are familiar with the eider for its soft downy feathers, used for years to make quilts, comforters, mattresses, and winter clothing. The female will pluck feathers from her breast to keep her nest warm. During the breeding season eiders frequent the coasts, living on a diet of mollusks and crustaceans.

Fer-de-lance in a pair of pants

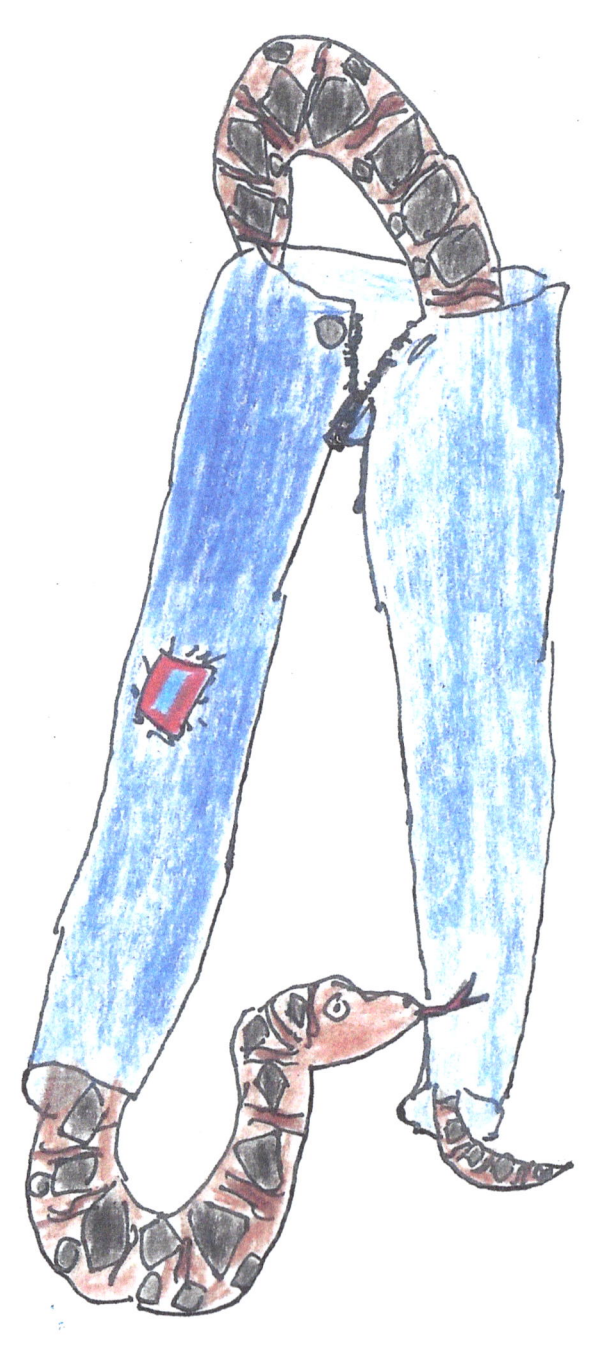

Fer-de-lance

This pit viper has been responsible for more deaths than any snake in the American tropics. The female gives live birth all at once to as many as 70 young snakes, each about a foot long and complete with venom (but hopefully in nobody's pants). The young are independent immediately after they are born. The name "fer-de-lance" is French for "iron of the lance."

Grison
in a prison

Grison

This handsome member of the weasel family lives mostly in South America and is sometimes kept as a pet. It has even been used to hunt chinchillas (a rodent with soft gray fur) just like its cousin, the ferret, has been used to hunt rabbits and rats.

Harrier
on a barrier

Harrier

Also known as the "marsh hawk," this bird of prey is unique among other hawks in that it relies on sound as well as sight when on the hunt. Its face is rounded like that of an owl's, and the stiff feathers around it help transmit sound.

Impala
at a gala

Impala

These graceful ungulates are not very likely to be found at your local Chevrolet® dealership, but rather the savanna and woodland edges in Africa. They are the most powerful jumpers of all antelopes, with the ability to leap ten feet in the air and travel up to 40 feet in one bound.

Jackdaw
with a hacksaw

Jackdaw

This dark gray relative of the crow has patches of lighter gray on the back and on the sides of the neck. Its other name "daw" may come from its call. The first half of its name may come from another word for "knave" or "rogue." This is a fitting term for this rascally bird, renowned for its thieving behavior.

Kodkod
in a hot rod

Kodkod

This small wildcat inhabits the central and southern areas of Chile and small areas of Argentina. Villagers on Chiloe Island in Southern Chile once thought "vampires" had raided their farms when livestock were found with bite marks on their necks. Further research revealed the real culprits: A pair of kodkods. The incident did not win the villagers' respect toward the wildcat; however, they also provide a great service by reducing the rodent populations.

Linsang
with a yin yang

Linsang

The banded linsang has beautiful markings, as do many other species of civet. They are skillful jumpers and climbers but they are just as much at home on the ground. Banded linsangs sleep in a nest of green vegetation during the day and hunt at night for insects, lizards, frogs, birds, and eggs.

Manatee at a vanity

Manatee

Most of this gentle aquatic "sea cow's" life is spent eating, sleeping, and migrating. A newborn manatee weighs from 25 to 80 pounds at birth and can swim alone within the first hour, even though the calf remains with its mother for almost two years.

Noctule
with a jewel

Noctule

This is one of the largest bats in Britain, with a head and body length of up to two inches and a wingspan averaging up to 14 inches. They can fly at 31 mph and have been known to fly over six miles from roosts to feeding areas. On hot days their metallic chirping may be heard from up to 700–1,000 feet away.

Oriole

The orioles of North America were named after those of the Old World. Those of the New World are more related to blackbirds. The most common of the Northern species, the Baltimore oriole, can reproduce with the Bullock's oriole, and for a time both were considered the same species and known as "Northern oriole." Recently, they were again separated into two species. These beloved songbirds can be attracted with orange slices, grape jelly, and occasionally nectar feeders.

Pangolin
playing a mandolin

Pangolin

The pangolin's pinecone-like scales protect it against its enemies when it rolls into a ball. When it cleans itself, it lifts the scales so its claws can reach the skin. It may also use its long slender tongue to reach any ants under there. Their tails serve great functions as well—as a club for defense, for balance when tearing into a termite mound, and the tree pangolin's tail even has a fingerlike tip to help it climb.

Queen
on a tureen

Queen

Like the monarch, the caterpillar of this butterfly feeds on milkweed to make itself distasteful to predators when it matures. This species of butterfly cannot tolerate very cold winters.

Rail
delivering mail

Rail

After nesting, the king rail molts and cannot fly for nearly a month. During courtship the male presents food to the female. The rail usually gets its food from the water, but if food is taken on land, this marsh bird will dunk it in water before eating it.

S erow
with a 'fro

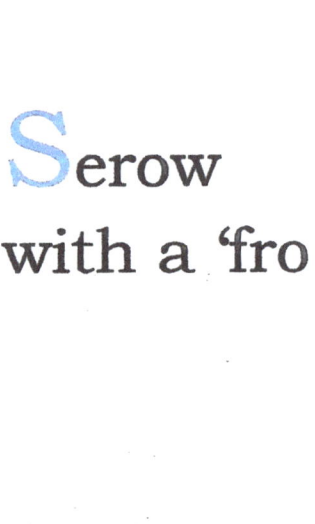

Serow

Serows use their climbing abilities to escape from predators or severe weather conditions. Both male and female have beards and small horns. The Japanese serow is the oldest living of the goat-antelopes. Their fossils, as well as those of similar animals, go back as far as the late Pliocene era.

T ogue

with a brogue

Togue

The name togue is believed to have originated from the Eastern Algonquian tribes, perhaps a shortened term of the Micmac name atoghwaasu. Togue spawn in autumn on the rocky gravel bottoms in the shallow waters. When the adult fish are ready to mate, they return to where they were spawned, like their salmon relatives do. Togue, lake trout, laker, or mackinaw—whatever you call them, these fish are strong fighters when hooked.

Urocyon
putting some tea on

Urocyon

Urocyon comes from the Greek "Uro" (tail) and "cyon" (dog). It is the genus of the gray fox (Urocyon cinereoargenteus). The species name cinereoargenteus (sin-oh-ree-ar-jen-tee-us/sin-oh-ree-o-ar-jen-toos) comes from the Greek meaning ash-colored and silver. There are 16 subspecies of Urocyon, including those living on six of California's eight Channel Islands. These foxes hunt alone for small mammals and birds, but fruits and vegetables are also on their menu. They are the only members of the dog family that can climb trees, which they do to hunt food and to "outfox" their enemies.

Vinegaroon with a balloon

Vinegaroon

Unlike other scorpions, the vinegaroon is considered non-venomous to humans but can still give a painful pinch. Its unusual name comes from the acid it emits from the base of its tail when threatened. Its whiplike appendage gives it its other name, "whip scorpion."

Weaver
with a fever

Weaver

The male baya weaver of Asia tries to attract his mates by only partially building nests. Once a female joins him, he may finish the nest, though the female often ends up with the task. While she is busy with the eggs, he goes to his other half-done nests to try and court a new girl.

Xerus
refusing to hear us

Yellowthroat

The male common yellowthroat resembles a bandit with its black facemask as it skulks about in its habitats of wetlands and thickets. The female has the olive brown and yellow plumage like the male but lacks the mask. The yellow-throated warbler (the names can be confusing as the yellowthroat is also a warbler) has a yellow throat as its name suggests, but is gray above with a white breast, and a black mask with streaks going down its sides.

Zoril
in something floral

Zoril

When this African mammal is alarmed, its first line of defense is to fluff itself up to look bigger. If that fails, it will turn and spray its enemy with a fluid even more foul-smelling than that of its American relatives, the skunks. Because of this defense mechanism it has been named one of the smelliest creatures on Earth.

Index

Mammals

Babirusa, Cavy, Drill, Grison, Impala, Kodkod, Linsang, Manatee, Noctule, Pangolin, Serow, Urocyon, Xerus, Zoril

Birds

Eider, Harrier, Jackdaw, Oriole, Rail, Weaver, Yellowthroat

Amphibians/Reptiles

Axolotl, Fer-de-lance

Fish

Togue

Insects/Arachnids

Queen, Vinegaroon

www.ingramcontent.com/pod-product-compliance
Lightning Source LLC
Chambersburg PA
CBHW041529070526
44586CB00002B/17